HOW TO WRITE A STORY...
ANY STORY

THE ART OF STORYTELLING

A directed approach
to writing great
fiction

BY
MICHAEL B. DRUXMAN

THE CENTER PRESS

How To Write A Story... Any Story:
The Art of Storytelling.
Copyright © 1997 by Michael B. Druxman

Acknowledgements

Grateful acknowledgement is made for permission to reprint photos from the following:

Abe Vigoda, in **Keaton's Cop**, 1990, Photo rights Courtesy of MGM Studios; Martin Sheen, and F. Murray Abraham, in **Dillinger and Capone**, 1995, Photo rights Courtesy of Concorde/New Horizons Pictures; Walter Hudson, in **Jolson**, 1996, Production at the Florida Studio Theater in Sarasota, Photo rights Courtesy of Reed Photography; Kelly Preston and Pato Hoffmann in **Cheyenne Warrior**, 1994, Photo rights Courtesy of Concorde/New Horizons Pictures; and Steve Kanaly in "Okavango", Photo rights Courtesy of Steve Kanaly.

Library of Congress Cataloging -in- Publication Data

Druxman, Michael B., 1941-
    How to write a story – any story: the art of storytelling/by
    Micahel B. Druxman.
    p.   cm.
    Filmography: p.
    Includes bibliographical references and index.
    ISBN 0-9626888-8-6 (alk. paper)
    1. Motion Picture authorship.   I. Title.
PN1996.D82 1997
808.2'3--dc21   97-18515
                                            CIP

Published by
        The Center Press
        30961 W. Aqoura Rd. Suite 223-B
        Westlake Village, CA 91361

Cover design: by Bart Design Associates
Book design: by Bart Design Associates
Printed in USA, by KNI

This book is dedicated to...

Michael Ansara
Henry Darrow
Steve Kanaly
Diane McBain
Jack Miller
Stanley Rubin

...and all my other show business friends who have continually encouraged me to keep on writ

TABLE OF CONTENTS

INTRODUCTION

Storytelling. It dates back to prehistoric times when fables were recited by tribe elders around campfires and men etched drawings on cave walls.

Today, the world is full of storytellers. They call themselves novelists, screenwriters, television writers, playwrights, short story writers and the like.

Each of these yarn-spinners works within his/her own unique format, aiming to please enthusiasts of that particular genre´ of writing. Novelists deal with the written word. Screenwriters and playwrights become specialists in both spoken dialogue and words destined to be converted into visual images.

Yet, whatever their area of expertise might be, all of them are doing exactly the same thing. They're telling a story.

As a writing instructor, I've found that many aspiring authors confuse format with story. They feel that, if they know the mechanics of how to write a screenplay or a novel, they automatically know how to tell a story.

Nothing could be further from the truth.

Awhile back, I had a young student who *desperately* wanted to be a screenwriter. He had a "great idea" for a film.   •

7

His movie would open in an artist's studio. The camera would begin in an overhead shot, moving down through the skylight to discover the artist/hero working on a canvas. Dissatisfied with the progress of his work, the artist leaves the studio, with the camera tracking behind him, and wanders the streets until he comes to a small, hidden away art supplies shop. There, from the elderly, somewhat strange proprietor, he purchases some paints and returns to his studio...camera still tracking him.

Back at his canvas, the artist finds that this new paint has an unusual texture to it. Indeed, whatever he paints, seems to take on a certain vibrancy.

The young student paused in his telling, and asked me what I thought.

"Interesting opening," I said. "Sounds like you might have something along the lines of *The Picture of Dorian Gray*."

"What's *The Picture of Dorian Gray?*"

I held back a sigh. "Never mind. What happens next?"

"I don't know."

"Well, how does it end?"

The youth shrugged. He hadn't the faintest idea.

He had an effective opening image. He knew how a camera should move. But, he had absolutely no idea as to how to develop a story.

Although this may seem like an extreme example, he's not alone. Even some of our most popular storytellers have had problems.

Several years ago, I had the privilege of interviewing master film-maker, Howard Hawks.

No question about it. In his time, Hawks made some great films. **Red River, His Girl Friday, Scarface, Sergeant York, Bringing Up Baby** and several other of his features are all-time classics. On the other hand, many of his pictures...particularly those that came later in his career...are a chore to watch. Despite their commercial success (thanks to the star presence of John Wayne), pictures like **Rio Bravo, Hatari, El Dorado** and **Rio Lobo** are rambling bores.

"Frankly," Hawks told me, "in making a film, I don't care that much about the story. I believe in making good scenes."

Certainly even the weakest of Hawks' pictures contain good scenes...memorable moments.

Remember the final shootout in **Rio Bravo?** John Wayne, Dean Martin, Walter Brennan and Ricky Nelson throwing lead and dynamite at the baddies. Great action! Had you cheering from the edge of your seat, right?

But did Hawks have to subject us to over two hours of tedium to get there?

Forget that **Rio Bravo** is considered a minor western classic. The picture is a bore. It's screenplay, a structural nightmare, is little more than a string of leisurely-paced scenes between Wayne and slinky Angie Dickinson, Wayne and spunky Ricky

Nelson, and Wayne and crotchety, old Walter Brennan.

Then, why is it so revered?

Primarily because of Hawks, who holds icon status close to that of John Ford. Wayne's presence naturally helps, and the final shootout, plus two or three amusing exchanges between the Duke and his drunken deputy, Dean Martin, are, indeed, memorable moments.

Yet, with a tightly written, well structured story, **Rio Bravo** could've been great. A western masterpiece like **High Noon** or **Shane**.

During most of his career, the late Mr. Hawks may have known how to make a good film, but in his later years when he had too much control over the writing of his pictures, he seemed to forget how to tell a story effectively.

That's the purpose of this book: To learn how to tell a *story effectively.* The lessons are relatively short and few. The techniques are easy to understand...and they can be applied to the great American novel, the blockbuster screenplay, or to any other area of storytelling one might wish to pursue.

So, let's get started.

I

WHAT'S IT ABOUT?

The spine of a story is its basic idea; an idea with a beginning, middle and end.

"What is **Gone With the Wind** about?"
I usually ask that question at the opening session of each of my classes. Semester after semester, the answers that I get are remarkably similar.
"It's about the Civil War."
Wrong. The Civil War is *background*. It's not what the story is about.
"It's a love story...about Scarlett and Rhett."
Again, wrong. That's a sub-plot. Indeed, *most* romantic relationships in stories are sub-plots.
"Scarlett and Ashley Wilkes?"
Another sub-plot. One, however, that provides a major motivation.
What is the *main storyline or spine of* **Gone With the Wind?**
"It's about Scarlett O'Hara."

11

Good answer. Elaborate, but keep it to one sentence.

"It's about the maturing of Scarlett O'Hara, from a capricious young girl to a knowing woman; set in the years before, during and after the Civil War."

Right on the button. The evolvement of Scarlett O'Hara is the dominant thread in the Margaret Mitchell novel and, also in David O. Selznick's great motion picture.

Important as they may be, Ashley, Rhett and everything else merely support that central premise or *spine*.

Let's try another one: **The Godfather.** I'm referring to the first film, featuring Marlon Brando as Vito Corleone and Al Pacino as son, Michael.

In **The Godfather**, who is the *central* character?

You have to know that before you can determine what the story is about.

If you answered, "Michael," you're right. Despite the fact that Brando has top billing, **The Godfather** is really Michael's story. So, what's it about?

That's right. It's <u>not</u> about the Mafia. That, like the Civil War in **Gone With the Wind**, is background.

It's not a love story. It's not a saga of court intrigue within the Corleone family, nor is it about wars between rival families. That is all sub-plot.

The Godfather is the story of the moral disintegration of Michael Corleone.

Why is Michael the central character in **The Godfather?**

Because it is Michael, not Vito, who is forced to act and/or make a fateful decision, as a result of the story's *climax.*

What is a story's *climax?*

Read the next chapters on Structure, and you'll find out.

As you may have surmised, the *central* character in a piece is not always the most visible character. In Robert Louis Stevenson's short classic novel, **Dr. Jekyll and Mr. Hyde**, for example, lawyer Utterson certainly has the largest role. But he is *not* the principal character. He is the *vehicle.* It is through his eyes that we view the central character, who, of course, is Dr. Jekyll.

Hopefully, you're getting the idea. Why don't you try a few on your own?

◆ ◆ ◆

EXERCISE: 1 . . . .

Jot down the *main storyline,* or spine of the following motion pictures:

[For the most part, we'll be using movies as examples, rather than novels, short stories or stage plays. That's because films are a more common experience. More of us have seen the same pictures than have read the same books or seen the same stage plays. And, *all* of the films we discuss are currently available on home video for your review.]

The African Queen

Witness

High Noon

Tootsie

Casablanca

The Maltese Falcon

Les Miserables

One Flew Over the Cuckoo's Nest

Guess Who's Coming to Dinner

The Odd Couple

When you've finished, you can compare your answers with mine on the following page.

◆ ◆ ◆

ANSWERS: . . . What Are They About?

The African Queen

During WWI, Charlie Allnut (Humphrey Bogart), a hard-drinking river boat captain, and Rose Sayer (Katharine Hepburn), a straight-laced lady missionary, join forces, journeying down a treacherous African river to torpedo a German gunboat.

Witness

John Book (Harrison Ford), a Philadelphia police detective, hides out from three corrupt brother officers on an Amish farm, while devising a plan to turn the tables on his pursuers.

High Noon

After a futile attempt to gain the help of his townspeople, Marshal Will Kane (Gary Cooper) must face four murderous outlaws alone.

Tootsie

When an out-of-work actor, Michael Dorsey (Dustin Hoffman), disguises himself as a woman, he achieves career success and also finds romance, but the pretense likewise creates for him many unforeseen predicaments.

Casablanca

Rick Blaine (Humphrey Bogart), sardonic expatriate American cafe´ owner, abandons his neutrality to help his former lover (Ingrid Bergman) and her Underground leader husband (Paul Henried) escape the Nazis.

The Maltese Falcon

Following the murder of his partner, detective Sam Spade (Humphrey Bogart) seeks the killer, learning that the mystery's solution is tied-in to the quest for a priceless art object by a group of peculiar and dangerous characters.

Les Miserables

Jean Valjean (Fredric March), an unfairly convicted and sentenced ex-convict who has created a new and honorable life for himself, is pursued through the years by Javert (Charles Laughton), a merciless police official.

One Flew Over the Cuckoo's Nest

MacMurphy (Jack Nicholson), a exuberant scalawag, is transferred for observation to a state mental hospital where he bolsters the spirits of the patients, while incurring the wrath of a deceptively vindictive ward nurse.

Guess Who's Coming to Dinner

Prominent, liberal San Francisco newspaper publisher Matt Drayton (Spencer Tracy) must scrutinize his own values when he learns that his daughter plans to marry a black man.

The Odd Couple

Slovenly Oscar and meticulous Felix (Walter Matthau and Jack Lemmon), two divorced poker-playing buddies, share the same apartment, and eventually wind up hating each other.

If you're still having problems determining the *spine*, you might ask yourself:

What does the central character want?

In the case of **Witness**, for instance, John Book wants to outwit and catch the bad guys.

In **The African Queen**, Charlie and Rose want to sink the German gunboat.

A correct answer to the question should lead you directly to the story's *spine*.

Now that you know what your story is about, the next step is to determine its structure.

II

YOUR MOST IMPORTANT LESSON
The Kick-Off

I always tell my students: "If you learn nothing else in this course, learn this."

The "this" to which I am referring is *story structure*, also known as *three-act structure*.

Three-act structure gives a story dramatic form, lucidity and balance. But its principle is not limited to stage plays. Indeed, *no story*, be it a novel, screenplay, dramatic television show, one-act stage play, short story or whatever, will work without a proper three-act structure. That is a given.

Indeed, the road to ruin is strewn with the bones of writers who defied three-act structure. Their manuscripts wound up in trash cans, bonfires, and at the bottom of canary cages.

Ignore three-act structure, and you will fail. I guarantee it.

Do I make my point?

There are six basic components to three-act structure. We'll examine each one individually but, for the record, they are:

- The Set-Up
- The Catalyst
- The First Turning Point
- The Climax
- The Final Confrontation
- The Resolution

On a graph, three-act structure looks like this:

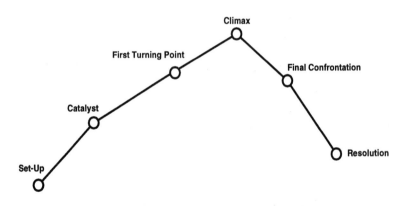

As you can see, three-act structure consists of both a rising and falling movement.

Everything begins with...

The Set-Up:

The purpose of the *set-up* is to give information. It acquaints the reader/viewer with the mood, setting and main character(s) of a narrative, and also gives him/her an idea as to what the direction or spine of the story might be.

In the set-up for **The African Queen**, Charlie Allnut brings the mail to the steamy, desolate native village, in which Rose Sayer and her brother have their religious mission. Out of politeness, the Sayers invite him to stay for tea. Allnut is hungover, unkempt and not well tutored on social graces. The Sayers, on the other hand, are very proper British. (At least, they're as proper as one can be in the African jungle.) Though each feels uncomfortable in the other's presence, we note that Rose is nicer to Charlie than her more stuffy brother.

During tea, Allnut tells the Sayers about the state of the European war (WW I), and how it may soon be encroaching on their isolated mission.

This is important information (or *exposition*) for both the Sayers and us. *They* learn of an approaching danger, while *we* gain knowledge that enables us to understand the unfolding story.

The Maltese Falcon also has an unadorned set-up.

Brigid Wonderly (Mary Astor) comes to the office of private detectives Sam Spade and Miles Archer, and hires them to get her sister away from a man named Floyd Thursby. We learn later that her story is a lie, but that's not important at this point.

What this opening scene accomplishes is to introduce us to the story's two most important characters, as well as two secondary ones. We get a feel for the leading character of Sam Spade, and his relationship to both his partner and secretary.

In other words, like the opening few minutes of ***The African Queen***, this set-up establishes the *status quo*.

The set-up in an average length screenplay (120 pages) will run between 1-15 pages. A novel's set-up takes much longer. The set-up for a short story would, of course, be less.

Actually, there's no set rule as to how long the set-up should take. In ***The Godfather***, which is an unusual case, the set-up is quite long, running somewhere around 30-40 minutes. It includes the wedding reception sequence, which introduces almost all of the major characters; the visit to Hollywood by attorney Tom Hagen (Robert Duvall), concluding with film producer Jack Woltz (John Marley) finding a horse's head in his bed[1]; and the meeting with drug dealer Sollozzo (Al Lettieri).

[1]This memorable Hollywood jaunt is an extraneous sequence, which has nothing to do with the story's spine. It's there as an illustration of what methods the Corleone family will use to achieve its aims.

Conversely, the classic **Bad Day at Black Rock** with Spencer Tracy has its set-up occurring *after* its *catalyst.*

That brings up your next question: "What is a catalyst?"

Read on, and I'll tell you.

The Catalyst:

The catalyst is the event that kicks off the story. It changes the status quo.

Perhaps the easiest illustration of a catalyst can be found in Irwin Allen's **The Poseidon Adventure.** Remember that disaster movie? Gene Hackman, Stella Stevens and a bunch of other surviving passengers were trying to escape an overturned ocean liner.

What was the catalyst?

The tidal wave that overturned the ship.

That's what changed the status quo.

How about **The Maltese Falcon?** What was the event that changed the status quo in that one?

Answer: The murder of Sam Spade's partner, Miles Archer.

After a gunshot sent ol' Miles tumbling down that embankment, the story became a murder mystery, with Sam Spade as one of the chief suspects.

The African Queen?

Its catalyst occurs right after Charlie departs the mission on his riverboat. The German army enters the village, burning it, enslaving the natives and brutalizing Rose's brother, who later dies.

As previously stated, *Bad Day at Black Rock* is one of those rare films that begins with its catalyst (i.e. Spencer Tracy getting off the train in the small desert town of Black Rock), then introduces us to all the characters as the story begins to unfold.

This reverse narration technique works well in **Bad Day at Black Rock** and a limited number of other stories, yet we would caution against its widespread use...primarily because it defeats a primary function of the set-up: To establish an empathy for the leading character(s).

I recall an unproduced screenplay I read several years ago, which opened with a family being robbed by a gang of crooks. The people in this family were the leading characters of the piece. We would follow their exploits throughout the film, however at the time of the robbery...with no set-up...we didn't know them from Adam. We had no reason to care about what happened to them.

The reverse opening in **Bad Day at Black Rock** works for several reasons, not the least of which is the warm, familiar on-screen persona of Spencer Tracy. Also, he's a mystery character. We don't know who he is, or why he's come to this town. And, finally, with the town populated with a bunch of anxious types, including veteran villains like Ernest Borgnine, Lee Marvin and Robert Ryan, we, as experienced moviegoers, know that Tracy has got to be the good guy.

Rule-of-thumb: Though there is no set length for a set-up, it's a good idea to introduce your catalyst and kick-off your story as soon as possible.

◆◆◆

EXERCISE: 2 . . . .

Now, on your own, list the catalysts for the following films:

North by Northwest

The Godfather

Gone With the Wind

Witness

The French Connection

The Searchers

◆◆◆

ANSWERS: . . . What is the Catalyst?

North By Northwest

Cary Grant is kidnapped, at gunpoint, out of the hotel lobby.

The Godfather

Marlon Brando is shot down in the street by members of a rival family.[2]

Gone With the Wind

The firing on Fort Sumter, reported at the Wilkes party, which begins the Civil War.

---

[2] Remembering that Michael is the story's central character or protagonist, this is the event that first gets him directly involved in Mafia activities. Prior to that, he was considered to be a "civilian," and took no part in his family's business.

Witness

The murder in the restroom, witnessed by the Amish boy.

The French Connection

Cops Gene Hackman and Roy Schieder observe a known hood in a nightclub and, because they have nothing better to do, follow him, thereby beginning their investigation.

The Searchers

John Wayne's brother's family is massacred by Indians, and niece Natalie Wood is kidnapped.

◆ ◆ ◆

As you can see, it was these events in each of these films which changed the status quo and kicked-off the story.

Next stop: The First Turning Point.

III

YOUR MOST IMPORTANT LESSON
A New Direction

The First Turning Point:

In every three-act play, about the end of the first act, the plot thickens. Complications arise. That is, an event occurs which gives the dramatic action fresh momentum, sending it off into a new direction.

This change in events is called the *First Turning Point.*

Two-act plays also have first turning points, as do one-acts. It's just easier to recognize them when you're dealing with three acts.

In Hitchcock's **North By Northwest,** the First Turning Point occurs when Cary Grant visits the United Nations building. He's being pursued by a gang of spies, who mistakenly believe that he is a government agent out to get them. And, because of his reputation as an irresponsible playboy, nobody...not the police, nor even his mother... will believe his story.

Grant has come to the UN to confront the man to whose house he was taken after he was kidnapped. As the man, a prominent statesman, is about to reveal some vital information to Cary, one of the spies throws a knife and kills him.

Cary pulls the knife out of the man's back. A photographer snaps a photo. And, guess what happens?

That's right! Poor Cary gets accused of the murder.

Why is this the First Turning Point?

Because, now, along with the spies, Cary has the law on his trail. He has no choice but to go undercover and run.

Let's look at *The Godfather.*

The First Turning Point in that epic occurs when, in the small Italian restaurant, Michael kills drug dealer Sollozzo and his crooked police captain companion, played by Sterling Hayden.

At that moment, by performing these executions, Michael makes an absolute commitment to his family's business. He is no longer a "civilian". He cannot go back. And, for the time being, he must flee to Sicily.

In *Witness,* we reach the First Turning Point when John Book is shot by the killer cop (Danny Glover) in the garage of his apartment building. Book now realizes that his superior (Josef Sommer), to whom he confided his knowledge of Glover's guilt in the restroom murder, is also implicated in the crime, and that he must play a lone hand. Taking Rachel (Kelly McGillis), the Amish woman, and her son with him, Book flees to her farm and hides out.

As you can see, in all three of these films, the First Turning Point forces the protagonist or hero[1] to make a fateful decision. It's that decision which keeps the story interesting.

◆ ◆ ◆

EXERCISE: 3 . . . .

What are the First Turning Points in the following?

Bad Day at Black Rock

The African Queen

---

[1]Conversely, the antagonist is the villain of the piece, or whatever force (human or not) that is opposing the protagonist.

White Heat

The Maltese Falcon

Gone With the Wind

Casablanca

Let's compare answers on the next page.

◆ ◆ ◆

ANSWERS: . . . What Are The First Turning Points?

Bad Day at Black Rock

Spencer Tracy visits the deserted farm of the Japanese farmer that he had come to see, and finds evidence that a body is buried there. This, and the fact that Ernest Borgnine tries to run him off the road on the way back to town, makes him realize that his life is in danger.

The African Queen

Rosie convinces Charlie that they should torpedo the German gunboat, and the journey down river begins.

White Heat

Cody Jarrett (James Cagney) pulls a surprise prison break, taking undercover officer Hank Fallon (Edmond O'Brien) along with him.[2]

[2]The catalyst for this gangster film had modern day outlaw Jarrett surrendering to authorities on a phony charge, as a way of beating a train robbery/murder rap for which he was being sought. Pretending to be a criminal, Fallon had entered prison and befriended Jarrett, hoping to get evidence to indict him for the train robbery. Watched closely by his F.B.I. colleagues, Fallon had been relatively "safe" in the prison, but the break puts him on the outside with Jarrett; on his own and, for the time being, forced to play Jarrett's game.

The Maltese Falcon

Joel Cairo (Peter Lorre) visits Sam Spade, seeking his help in retrieving the black bird. This is the first time that Spade has heard about the Falcon, the search for which turns out to be the primary motivation behind all the murder and mayhem in the story.

Gone With the Wind

Scarlett, returning to Tara as a refugee, finds it barren. She learns that her mother has died, and that her father is losing his mind. Forced by these circumstances to become the head of her family, she vows: "As God is my witness, I'll never be hungry again".

Casablanca

Ugarte (Peter Lorre) is arrested, and the stolen letters of transit[3] fall under Rick's control.

◆ ◆ ◆

From this point, your story continues to develop until it reaches its Climax.

---

[3]The theft of the letters from the German couriers was the story's catalyst.

IV

YOUR MOST IMPORTANT LESSON
The Climax and Beyond

What is a *Climax?*

Naturally, I mean in the dramatic sense.

According to Webster, it's "the point of greatest intensity".

In other words, the *culmination.*

It's the point in a story where events have developed to such a degree that all issues must now be resolved.

It is the circumstance which accelerates the action and prompts the protagonist and/or the antagonist to act.

It is their moment of decision.

In **High Noon,** the climax is reached when the clock strikes twelve, and the train whistle is heard in the distance. To Marshal Will Kane, this means that the last of the killers have arrived in town. There is no more time to seek help from the townspeople, who have already turned their backs on him.   He must now go out into street and meet his fate.

The climax in **The Godfather** comes with the death of Vito Corleone (Marlon Brando). This unexpected *happening makes Michael* (Al Pacino) the absolute head of the Corleone family, yet he knows that he must act decisively if he is to solidify that position.

Final Confrontation:

Many people have a problem distinguishing between the climax and the *Final Confrontation*.

Remember the classic Burt Lancaster/Kirk Douglas western, **Gunfight at the O.K. Corral?** That's the one that recreated the infamous Wyatt Earp/Doc Holiday clash with the Clanton brothers in Tombstone, Arizona.

What was the climax of that picture?

No, it wasn't the gunfight. That shoot-out was the final confrontation.

The climax takes place a few minutes earlier in the film, when Wyatt Earp's younger brother is ambushed one night and shot down in the street by the Clantons. It is that dastardly deed that makes the elder Earp take action and finally go after his enemies.

The same can be said for **High Noon**. The final confrontation in that picture is the shoot-out between Will Kane and the Frank Miller gang.

The final confrontation in **The Godfather** is also a bloodbath. While Michael is in church for the christening of his nephew, his lieutenants are out assassinating the heads of the rival families, thereby solidifying his position as the most powerful Mafia head.

Thus, the *climax* is the event which elicits the final confrontation.

The climax is the cause. The final confrontation is the effect.

Resolution:

This brings us to the *Resolution*, which is the wrap-up... the tag... the final outcome of your story.

Does boy get girl?

Does the wounded hero live?

What was the killer's motive?

These are the kinds of questions that are cleared up with your resolution.

John Huston's ***The Treasure of the Sierra Madre*** is resolved by nature...when the two surviving prospectors (Walter Huston and Tim Holt) discover that their hard earned gold dust has blown back to the place from which it came.

In ***High Noon***, following the shoot-out, a disgusted Marshal Kane throws down his badge and leaves town with his wife.

The Godfather resolves itself with Michael lying to his wife that he was not responsible for his brother-in-law's murder, then being accepted by his lieutenants as the new "Godfather".

A couple words of advice:

1) The nearer your climax is to your final confrontation, the stronger your ending is going to be, and
2) The shorter your resolution, the better.

◆ ◆ ◆

EXERCISE: 4.

Now, list the
     a) climax
     b) final confrontation
     c) resolution
in each of the following motion pictures.

Gone With the Wind

The Maltese Falcon

White Heat

Casablanca

Witness

The African Queen

41

♦ ♦ ♦

ANSWERS: . . . Here are the CLIMAX, etal.

Gone With the Wind
a.) Melanie (Olivia de Havilland) dies, leaving husband Ashley (Leslie Howard) free. Yet, now that her long time love is available, Scarlett realizes that it is really Rhett that she wants.

b.) Scarlett goes to Rhett, professes her love, but he walks out on her, stating, "Frankly, my dear, I don't give a damn."

c) Scarlett decides to return to Tara, where she will devise a plan to get Rhett back. "After all," she says, "tomorrow is another day."

The Maltese Falcon
a) The black bird is delivered to Sam Spade's apartment, and it is discovered to be a fake. Cairo and Guttman (Sydney Greenstreet) resolve to continue their search for the real artifact.

b) Spade accuses Brigid of Archer's murder, and she confesses.

c) Spade turns Brigid over to the police.

White Heat
a) During the robbery of a chemical plant, a member of Jarrett's gang recognizes Fallon as a cop. Fallon turns his weapon on the gang members, but he is subdued.

b) The authorities arrive, and a shoot-out ensues, in which all the gang members, except Jarrett, are killed. Fallon escapes Jarrett.

c) Trapped on the top of a huge chemical storage tank, Jarrett shouts, "Made it, Ma! Top of the World!" Then, the tank explodes and he is blown to bits.

Casablanca

a) Victor Lazlo (Paul Henried) is arrested in Rick's cafe´.

b) Rick tricks Chief Renault (Claude Rains) into freeing Lazlo, then at the airport, he shoots Major Strasser (Conrad Veidt).

c) Rick sends Ilsa off with Lazlo on the Lisbon plane. Rick and Renault decide to go fishing.

Witness

a) John Book hits a bully who was accosting one of the peaceful Amish. The incident is observed by the local sheriff, who now knows where Book is hiding out, and reports this information to the crooked Philadelphia cops.

b) Book and the crooked Philadelphia cops shoot it out on the Amish farm.

c) Realizing that he and Rachel (Kelly McGillis) can never have a life together, Book returns to Philadelphia.

The African Queen
a) While trying to torpedo the German gunboat, the African Queen sinks during a storm.
b) Charlie and Rose are rescued by the Germans. As they are about to be hung as spies, the gunboat hits the half-submerged African Queen, and is sunk.
c) Charlie and Rose escape the sinking German craft, and swim off to freedom.

Inevitably, in every one of my Storytelling classes, I find at least one student who "fights" me on the concept of three-act structure.

"Why does there have to be a catalyst?" they ask. Or, "Why a first turning point?"

The best way to answer that sort of question is with another question:

What would happen if just one of those elements was missing from a particular story?

Take the catalyst out of ***The Poseidon Adventure***, and what do you have?

A travelogue about an uneventful ocean voyage.

Don't kidnap Cary Grant in ***North By Northwest***, and we'll be stuck with a dull business meeting, followed by an evening at the theatre with him and his mother.

No first turning point in ***Witness?***

Then, how is John Book going to get to Rachel's farm?

And, as far as the climax is concerned, if the train never arrives in **High Noon**, there's not going to be any gunfight, is there?

As I said earlier, ignore three-act structure, and you will fail.

That is a given.

V

A MATTER OF CHARACTER

Now that you've structured your story, it's time to concentrate on the people who will populate it.

Actually, many writers...including this one...often begin with the characters.

That's what I enjoy most about writing. The people. Putting them down onto the printed page.

I'll see somebody on the street that catches my interest. There's something unique about them that intrigues me, or maybe they remind me of someone that I once knew. But whatever the case, I make a mental note, and sooner or later they wind up in something that I write.

Just recently, I was lunching with my agent in a restaurant. I noticed a man sitting behind him. He was probably in his late twenties, and had a jolly, friendly face. He was also fat...so fat that his bare belly burst out from the bottom of his yellow T-shirt and spilled over his belt. [Incidentally, he was an *outie*.]

The restaurant was doing an "all you can eat" promotion, and this guy was eating barbecued ribs...plate after plate of them. Barbecue sauce covered his chin, and dripped down to stain his shirt. But, he didn't care. He was in food heaven.

I watched with growing fascination as he devoured that meal, totally unaware of the spectacle he was making of himself, and I thought: "This guy is disgustingly beautiful. He'd make a great character for a movie."

I don't know where or in what it's going to be, but somewhere I'm going to use that fat fellow. He has become a member of my mental pool of characters.

The better you *know* your characters, the more three-dimensional they're going to be.

"Do your characters *have* to be three-dimensional?"

Believe it or not, a student once asked me that question.

My answer: "If you want your reader/viewer to care about your characters.... If you want them to be *credible*... then, yes, they <u>must</u> be three-dimensional."

So, *how* do you get to know your characters, so that they become three-dimensional?

One useful method is to write a biography of them, using information that you fill in on <u>The Three Dimensional Character Chart</u> located at the end of this chapter.

I imagine that you're asking yourself: "Do I have to know *all* that about my character *before* I can begin writing?"

No. Not necessarily. However, the more specific and in-depth information you have about a character, the better you'll understand him. Then the more "real" he (or she) will become.

You have to know what makes this person you're writing about "tick".

Put it another way:

Every character has a demon...some psychological insecurity... big or little...that grates on their personalities, influencing their every day lives.

You have one. I have one. We all have one.

I'm talking about the kind of irritating personality quirk or mental liability that makes psychiatrists rich.

The shrinks tell us that these quirks are formed in us by the time we're five.

That's why it's so important to create a family background for your important characters. Understand how their parents affected them and you begin to understand your character.

For example, if Joey's mother is always telling him that he's doing something wrong, he may grow up into an adult who has trouble making decisions because he's afraid of making mistakes.

Maybe little Mary's parents were always arguing at home, so she found comfort by going to the movies. As an adult, she might continue to avoid conflict by escaping to the movies or television.

This aspect of her personality, however, doesn't have to be so overwhelming that it controls Mary's life. It can also manifest itself as just a quirky trait, such as an unusual interest in a particular movie star[1], or an addiction to a certain television soap opera[2].

Perhaps the two most important questions to ask about your character are:

1. What does he want?
2. What is he afraid of?

Answer those, and you're well on your way to knowing that person...and what makes him "tick".

And, if you know what makes him "tick," you are less likely to violate that character.

What is a *character violation?*

I'll answer that with a personal example.

Awhile back, I was writing a fictional screenplay[3] in which my leading character was John Dillinger, the infamous bank robber of the 1930s.

[1] In **Alice Doesn't Live Here Anymore**, star Ellen Burstyn had adored the legendary Alice Faye since she was a child.
[2] In **Rain Man**, Dustin Hoffman's Raymond finds security in his daily viewings of "The People's Court".
[3] A somewhat revised verson of my original script was filmed under the title of **Dillinger and Capone** (1995).

In my original storyline, Dillinger wanted to steal a large amount of money that was kept in a secret basement safe. I planned to have him sneak into the basement at night, blow open the safe and escape.

When I got close to writing that scene, which occurred just over halfway into the script, I hit a tremendous writer's block. I'd sit down to work, and found that I couldn't write a word. This went on for about two weeks.

Instinctively, I knew that there was something amiss with my story, but I couldn't pinpoint the exact problem. Then, one morning, I woke up and immediately knew what was wrong.

Martin Sheen was legendary outlaw John Dillinger in **Dillinger And Capone** (1995). According to this revised version of historical record, the FBI killed the wrong man in front of Chicago's Biograph Theater in 1934, and the real Dillinger has retired to farm and family life... until summoned back to the criminal world by Al Capone.

Academy Award-winner F. Murray Abraham played Al Capone, the former "King of Chicago," in **Dillinger And Capone** (1995). Set in the early 1940s after his release from prison for tax evasion charges, the film finds Capone teetering on verge of madness, due to the effects of advanced syphilis.

I had violated the character of John Dillinger. The fact is that Dillinger was not a burglar. He did not sneak in through the "back door".

He was a daring bank robber. He got a thrill out of walking into a bank, guns drawn, and saying, "I'm John Dillinger. This is a hold-up!"

My having Dillinger blow the safe at night was against his nature. It was not true to his real character.

Once I realized this, the remainder of my screenplay flowed very quickly.

Now, create your own character...one that you'll want to work with later on in this manual.

Answer all the questions on <u>The Three Dimensional Character Chart</u>, and watch that person spring to life.

THREE DIMENSIONAL CHARACTER CHART

General Information

Name: Sex:

Age: Birthday: Birthsign:

Birthplace: Nationality:

Religion:

Feelings About Religion:

Languages Spoken:

Political Party:

Class in Society: Lower   Middle   Upper

Morals: Ambitions:

Education:

Name of School: Where:

Date Graduated:

Marital Status:

Physical Appearance

Height: Weight: Eyes: Hair:

Mouth: Lips: Eyebrows: Jawline:

Hands: Fingers: Shoulders: Limbs:

Complexion: Face: Forehead: Breasts:

Waist: Hips: Neck: Ears:

Nose: Teeth: Birthmarks: Scars:

Body Type: Posture: General Appearance:

Family Background

Father: Profession: Live/Dead

Relationship with Father?

Mother: Profession: Live/Dead

Relationship with Mother?

Were Parents Happily Married?

Were Parents Divorced?

Step-Parents?   Relationship with Step-Parents?

Brothers (number):   Sisters (number):

Relationship with Siblings?

Was Home Life Happy?

Unique Information Regarding Family:

Occupation/Profession

Profession:

Union:

Education in Work:

Favorite Subjects (School):

Hours Worked:

Poorest Subjects (School):

Quality of Work Performed:

Grades Completed (School):

Income:

Reputation:

Military Service

Branch:

Nationality:

Enlisted Rank:

Highest Rank Achieved:

Service Dates:

Unit or Legion:

Served Under What Ruler:

Campaigns:

Decorations:

Ability as a Soldier:

Personal Information

Hobbies/Pastimes:

Favorite Books: Favorite Magazines:

Favorite Newspaper: Favorite Records:

Taste in Jewelry: Favorite Colors:

Favorite Entertainment: Favorite Clothes:

Favorite Foods: Favorite Drinks:

House (Type):   Apartment:

City Background?   Country Background?

Describe Furnishings (Use colors & materials):

Selection (Type) of Men/Women:

Character Trait Analysis

Major Traits: Minor Traits:

Outstanding Qualities: Inferior Qualities:

Habitual Expressions: Habitual Mannerisms:

Fears: Frustrations:

Complexes: Temperament:

Emotions: Attitude Toward Life:

Leader?   Follower?   Dropout?

VI

CHARACTER REVELATIONS

People reveal themselves through their words.

They tell us things that they want us to know. And, to the careful listener, they disclose things about themselves that they don't realize they're revealing.

I'll give you an example. The following is an excerpt from my one-man stage play, *Jolson*, dealing with Al, the "Mammy" man of *The Jazz Singer* fame.

The play is set during the filming of *The Jolson Story* by Columbia Pictures. Unhappy with the performance of Larry Parks in the title role, Al Jolson has caused a disturbance and been ejected from the set.[1] He returns to his dressing room, and speaks to the audience:

---

[1] That's another important point to remember: A character always enters a scene from another scene, whether it was played off-stage or on. Thus, his attitude and mood in the current scene will be affected by what transpired in the previous one.

JOLSON

I don't believe it.

Columbia's spending over two-and-a-half
million to film my life story and they're
gonna wind up with tinif...a piece of crap.

I should've made the deal with Warner
Brothers. At least, I own a piece of
that joint.

(Paces)

Larry Parks as Jolie! Hah!!

The kid can't move from the waist
down. His tochis is dead.

I wanted Cagney.

(Ponders a moment)

Hell, I wanted me.

They said I wouldn't be convincing as a
twenty year old.

There was a joke floating around the
set yesterday: How can you tell Parks
and me apart in blackface?

When we get down on our knees, he can
get up.

New York actor Walter Hudson was Al in the one-person play, *Jolson,*
which opened its first professional production at the Florida Studio
Theater in Sarasota in November, 1996.

•••

I didn't think it was funny.

>   *(Crosses to dressing table. Picks*
>   *up phone.)*

This is Jolie. Get me Harry Cohn.

>   *(To audience)*

The kid's mouthing my singing okay,
but he don't move like me.

I try to coach him.

But, Mr. Green, our shmuck director, says
I'm holding up production.

(Into phone:)

Yeah, honey? He's expected momentarily?
Tell him to call me in my dressing room.

(Hangs up; Sudden thought.)

Jessel!!

(Paces; to audience:)

You think he's behind this? Telling
people I'm a troublemaker or something?

That putz would love to see this movie
go into the toilet.

My "friend"!!

He's stewing because they're filming my
life and not his.

He'd do anything to throw a monkey wrench
into the works.

Why shouldn't he? I've stuck it to him
enough times.

You hear what he did?

Smart guy! He's over at Fox producing
important pictures like The Dolly
Sisters with Betty Grable...and one day

60

he disappears. Zanuck's looking all
over for him: "Where's Georgie? Maybe
we should call the cops."

Turns out he's in Chicago. Got an
offer to do one week at the Oriental
and he took it.

Can you imagine? A million dollar
picture's rolling and he's standing on some
stage trying to impersonate me and saying...

> *(Imitates Jessel.)*

"Hello, Mama....This is Georgie. You
know, the one who sends the check every month."

> *(To audience; incredulous.)*

People <u>pay</u> to see him do that!?!

> *(To himself:)*

Jolie, you're getting crazy. Jessel's
at Fox. Harry Cohn wouldn't even take
his phone calls....Relax.

> *(PHONE RINGS. Jolson dashes for the phone;*
> *grabs it.)*

Harry?

You been talkin' to Jessel?

You wouldn't even take his phone
calls....I didn't think so.

Sorry, if you want to know what happens next, you're going to have to read or see the play.

But, what's Jolson doing there?

On the surface, he's merely airing his grievances, yet he's also expressing a strong undercurrent of paranoia, jealousy and fear.

If you said that to Al, he'd certainly deny it, but those emotions are most definitely there.

At any rate, this should give you a pretty good idea of what I'm talking about, so now sit down and write your own monologue for the character that you created in the previous chapter. Let him/her reveal his/her inner self without knowing it.

Good luck!

VII

PEOPLE WILL TALK

Dialogue.

It's one of the two afflictions that always seem to plague writers.[1]

The dictionary defines dialogue as: "a conversational passage in a play or a narrative," and/or "an exchange of ideas or opinions."

Now, writers are usually bright people. They have ideas, opinions. And, they know how to talk.

So, why can't they put their talking down onto a piece of paper?

Why don't their character's words sound real? Natural?

Perhaps these writers simply don't listen. They don't know how people sound.

[1] The other is plotting, which will be discussed later.

Personally, I find dialogue to be one of the easiest aspects of my writing.

Of course, the people who live with me think I'm a bit balmy when they walk by my work area and hear me talking to myself.

But, I'm just acting out my dialogue; testing the words I've written to see how they sound when they're spoken aloud. And, I always speak them in character...accents and all.

How do I know how my character will sound?

Knowing where he comes from helps. Also, his age. His level of education.

And, if he/she is a real person, I listen to any existing recordings of his/her voice.

Finally, I fix or create that character's voice inside my head, then when I write them a line of dialogue, I hear *them* say it.

Some wise man (or woman) once said that there were three reasons...and *only three*...to justify putting a line of dialogue into a script, and if a particular line doesn't fulfill one or more of those reasons, then you should eliminate it.

What are the reasons?
- To further the plot.
- To develop or reveal character.
- To get a laugh.

I think that may be the most important lesson one can learn about writing dialogue.

On the other hand, there are several common mistakes a struggling writer will make when creating his dialogue:

1. Redundancy.
   Saying it once is usually enough.
2. Individual lines are too long.
   People are lazy. They don't usually give lengthy discourses.
3. Speeches are stilted.
   People use slang and contractions.
4. All characters talk the same.
   People have different pattens of speech.

Thus, for more natural dialogue, keep the following points in mind:

1. People do not always finish their thoughts or sentences. Or, they may finish a thought after injecting another thought.

2. People do not always respond *directly* to another person.

3. People often repeat the same sentence, idea or word.

4. People speak in words and phrases, not always in complete sentences.

5. People do not always speak grammatically correct.

6. People use phrases characteristic of them, such as "You know," or "As a matter of fact...".

7. People speak differently under stress.

In their attempts to write natural dialogue, some writers overdo it. Their dialogue is *so* natural that it becomes boring.

Remember, if you want to write good dialogue:

8. Keep the informal aspects of your scene to a minimum. Flavor you words *just enough* to create an *illusion* of familiarity , but don't inundate us with it.

9. Get to the point.

10. A final suggestion: Act out your scenes into a tape recorder, then play them back. What sounds real and what doesn't should become readily apparent.

◆ ◆ ◆

EXERCISE: 5 . . . .

Now, write a short scene between the character you've created and an authority figure, such as a teacher, employer, parent, policeman, or what-have-you.

Then, read it aloud...into a tape recorder, if possible...and hear how it sounds.

And, don't forget to include conflict in your scene.

What's Conflict!?!

If you don't know, then maybe you'd better hold off tackling this assignment until after you finish reading the next chapter.

VIII

CONFLICT & PLOTTING

Conflict:

It's the basis of all drama.

Conflict is what makes your story and scenes interesting.

The dictionary defines conflict as "a clash of opposing ideas, interests and so forth; a disagreement."

Thus, in your story, the way to define the conflict is to answer two rather simple questions:
1. What does your hero/heroine want?
2. Who or what is stopping he/she from getting it?

Every scene you write should have a conflict...even if it's a friendly one.

How can you have a "friendly" conflict? Try this out.

> "Honey, where do you want to go for dinner tonight?"
> "How about that Chinese place?"
> "I'm tired of Chinese. Let's go to the steak house?"
> "That dump!?!...I was really looking forward to some eggrolls."
> "There's eggs and rolls in the frig. I'll even mix 'em up for you. But, <u>no</u> Chinese!"

Since nobody's punching or shooting the other party (yet), *that's* a "friendly" conflict.

I think it was Neil Simon who said that the easiest way to create conflict in your story is to put two diverse characters together in the same room, then watch the sparks fly.

Certainly that's what he did with slovenly Oscar and finicky Felix in *The Odd Couple.*

The same principle applies to Rose and Charlie in *The African Queen*, or to *Dr. Jekyll and Mr. Hyde.*

Of course, in the case of the good doctor, you've got two disparate personalities occupying the same body, rather than the same room.

Ergo, you don't have to have a conflict with another person or thing. In this case, you have an inner conflict working for you.

That's what I've had to contend with in the writing of my one-person plays, such as *Jolson.*

Since the actor is on stage by himself, he has to be experiencing an internal struggle, examining his past life to see how he arrived at this point of crisis.

Plotting:

For me, plotting is the hardest aspect of writing a screenplay. I get off on the dialogue. I love

Steve Kanaly was cast as white hunter J.D. Helms in "Okavango," a syndicated African-adventure series, which aired on Fox's F/X cable channel.

playing with interesting characters, but, in a plot oriented story[1], it's like pulling teeth for me to decide what happens next.

Coming up with a fantastic opening and a sure-fire ending are fairly easy. It's determining what comes in between that keeps me up nights.[2]

To be able to properly plot your story, you *must* know how it ends before you get there. In a character piece, that ending can be a little on the general side[3] , but in a plot-oriented story, especially mysteries, you must know *precisely* what your solution is, because that solution motivates everything that comes before it.

Once you know where you're going with your story, it becomes a matter of getting your characters from point A to point Z, in not necessarily the straightest route possible.

---

1 Mysteries and thrillers are usually plot-oriented, while comedies (***Moonstruck, When Harry Met Sally...***) are often character driven.

2 The most effortless experience I've ever had in plotting scripts, was when I wrote episodes for "Okavango," an African-adventure series that starred Steve Kanaly. The producer of that syndicated show insisted that each segment be mapped-out scene-by-scene *before* I actually started writing. When I finally sat down at the computer, it was virtually a matter of just "connecting-the-dots" to complete the teleplay. True, much spontaneous creativity was sacrificed, but the work went *very* quickly.

3 Sometimes, *particularly* in a character piece, your emerging characters will dictate an entirely new conclusion than you had originally envisioned. *They* decide the direction of the story, and, when that happens, it can be the most exciting part of the writing experience.

In ***Casablanca***, for example, the screenwriters knew that the story had to end one of two ways. Ingrid Bergman would wind up with either Humphrey Bogart or Paul Henreid. That was their "general" ending. Fortunately, the plot lent itself to keeping the *final* answer to that question vague until they actually had to write the concluding scene, set at the airport.

You've got to throw some obstacles (i.e. conflicts) into their path, and those obstacles should have a reason for being there, other than for the writer's convenience[4].

We, as the reader/viewer, don't have to know those reasons at the time that the obstacle presents itself, but by the end of the story, those reasons must be crystal clear.

For example, from the very beginning of **Bad Day at Black Rock**, we sense that the townspeople have something to hide from Spencer Tracy, but we don't learn until later exactly *why* they are afraid of him. Once we do know, however, the motivation for all of their previous actions becomes obvious.

The same applies for any good mystery. In **The Maltese Falcon**, we don't know *why* Sam Spade's partner, Archer, was killed at the start of the film until, at the finish, Bogart accuses Mary Astor of the murder and she confesses. Once she tells him her reason for shooting Archer, everything, like the final piece of a complicated jigsaw puzzle, falls into place. It all makes sense.

---

4 "Oh," the hack writer says, "I need an action scene here. I'll throw in a car chase."

Car chases in movies are really a bit overdone. Indeed, that massively destructive pursuit through the streets of San Francisco in **The Rock** (1996), plot wise, had no valid reason to be there. If you must put a car chase into your story, make sure you know who is chasing who and *why*.

Like with a line of dialogue, every scene you write must have one of three reasons for being in your script:

- To further the plot.
- To develop or reveal character.
- To get a laugh.[5]

If your scene doesn't fulfill one of those purposes, then it's superfluous. Take it out. It will only slow down the forward action of your story.

That can be a painful process. More than once, usually after I've been playing around with a character that I've fallen in love with, I've had to force myself to eliminate a favorite scene from my script because there was no good justification for its being there.

True story (AKA: "The Best Laid Plans...."): I've always prided myself on being able to supply sufficient motivation to justify all actions in my scripts. I'm almost a fanatic about it. Truly, read one of my screenplays and you will see how I get from A to Z.

A few years ago, I sold **Keaton's Cop**, one of my original screenplays, to an independent producer-director, who for his own reasons, decided to rewrite it himself.[6]

The story was an action mystery/comedy, in which each scene had a particular and necessary purpose.

[5] If this is the sole purpose of your scene, better keep it very funny and very short.
[6] Certainly that is not an unusual practice in the ego driven world of movie-making.

In one scene, the detective visits the home of a witness and, while there, learns a vital piece of information that leads to his solving the mystery. The scene concludes with the bad guys shooting a rifle grenade into the house and the witness being killed in the explosion...leading to a wild car chase.

In the producer-director's re-write, the action elements of the scene were virtually untouched, however the line of dialogue that conveyed the important clue was eliminated.

Therefore, the only viable reason for that scene being in the picture no longer existed.

Later, when the detective "solves" the mystery, you have absolutely no idea how he knows what he knows.

Truly, I cringe every time I see that scene.

Major films can suffer from the same problem. Consider the film *In the Heat of the Night*, the 1967 Academy Award winning (Best Picture, Actor, Screenplay) classic starring Sidney Poitier and Rod Steiger that later became the basis for a hit television series.

I love this picture. I've seen it many times. I even own it on laser disc. But, for the life of me, I still don't know how Sidney Poitier, playing homicide detective Virgil Tibbs, solves the murder.

You don't believe me?

Take another look at the film.

There's not one scene in the movie that gives Poitier information which would help him to link the murder of the wealthy businessman to actress

Quentin Dean's unwanted pregnancy and illegal abortion at the end of the movie. Yet, he does it.

Years ago, I met John Ball, author of the original novel, at a social gathering. I asked him about this omission.

Admitting that it was a painful subject, he told me that the scene in question was in his original novel and, he believed, in the screenplay adaptation by Stirling Silliphant. But, somewhere along the line, director Norman Jewison decided that, for whatever reason, that scene was unnecessary and it was cut.

All this reminds me of those remarks from Howard Hawks that I shared with you earlier.

Directors make interesting scenes.
Writers tell stories.

A final word about plotting:
Avoid coincidence.
Motivation. That's the key to all good plotting.

◆◆◆
EXERCISE: 6 . . . .

Now, write that scene which we talked about at the end of the last chapter. Remember to add conflict as well as some information that might lead into or motivate a subsequent scene.

IX

EXPOSITION

What *is* exposition?

According to the dictionary, it's "the presentation of information in clear, precise form."

Translating that into storytelling terms, it's the process of giving the reader or viewer the important background facts he needs to know in order to understand what is going on in your novel, play or screenplay.

As we said in an earlier chapter, the most crucial exposition is often delivered during your Set-Up.

Remember *The African Queen*?

Charlie is invited by Rose and her brother to stay for tea and, while there, he informs them about the European War (i.e. WW1).

That's exposition.

Exposition, unfortunately, is a necessary evil.

Improperly presented, it can stop your forward action and turn your scene into an absolute bore.[1]

The key is to make it interesting.

How can you accomplish that?

One of the best things you can do is to have something else going on in your scene while your characters are delivering their "vital" information. Create an unrelated minor conflict.

A perfect example of this kind of diversion can be found in **The Enemy Below**, (1957) a first-rate submarine chase movie that stars Robert Mitchum and Curt Jurgens. It's available on tape, so take a look at it.

Mitchum plays the new captain of a Navy destroyer during WW2. Before he even appears on screen, there's an amusing scene in the officer's lounge, in which four of the officers are playing Bridge. Unhappily, one of the older men is stuck with an inexperienced Ensign as his Bridge partner. The anxious young man keeps making erroneous bids or playing the wrong card.

It's during this bantering across the card table that the officers trade scuttlebutt about their new captain who'd come aboard late the night before and is now asleep.

A few years ago, I wrote a yet unproduced screenplay, entitled **Aunt Addie**, which illustrates the same point.

---

[1] "Look, guys, here's what the movie's all about...."

The story is set in New York City in 1939. Lezak is a Nazi agent. His U.S. contact is Mrs. Brenner, an overweight woman who runs a bakery. This scene, which begins on page 35 of the script, takes place in the back of her shop.

Mrs. Brenner is rushing about, getting her breads, cookies and Danish ready for the day's business. Lezak sits at a table, drinking coffee and eating a feast of strudel. He is tired and irritable.

> LEZAK
> ....It was all arranged that the ship
> wouldn't be allowed to dock in Cuba,
> or the South American countries. But,
> this decision by Roosevelt wasn't planned.

> MRS. BRENNER
> Yah, the papers were full of it.

She notices that he has almost finished eating the strudel on his plate.

> MRS. BRENNER
> (Continuing)
> You like the strudel?

> LEZAK
> (Trying to be polite)
> It's very nice.

> MRS. BRENNER
> Good. Try one with raisins.

She grabs another strudel from her tray and plops it
down on the plate in front of him. He's really had
his fill.

> LEZAK
>
> No... thank you... I...

> MRS. BRENNER
>
> Eat. Then I give you a bed in the
> back, and you will sleep.

Lezak is too tired to protest. He picks at the strudel,
as he tries to regain his train of thought. He does
not like this doting woman.

> LEZAK
>
> If only these simple-minded Americans
> had done what we expected... allow the
> ship entry and accept the filthy Jews....
> Perhaps the Americans are getting smarter...
> starting to realize that these swine can
> only destroy their country.

> MRS. BRENNER
>
> Nein. They are still stupid. It was
> a political decision.

> LEZAK
>
> With those children, I could have
> walked by immigration, and nobody
> would have noticed.

> MRS. BRENNER
> But, last night, why not leave them on
> the ship?

> LEZAK
> For an "Uncle" to abandon his nephew
> and niece would create questions....
> Also, these Jew children would have
> been useful on my mission.

> MRS. BRENNER
> Now you must do it without them.
> (Notes that he's hardly
> touched his raisin strudel)
> Eat your strudel.

> LEZAK
> (Snaps at her)
> Enough with the strudel!

He flings the strudel across the table. She is
shocked at his outburst, but then he continues,
embarrassed:

> LEZAK
> (Continuing)
> I must retrieve the microfilm.

And the scene goes on from there.

Hopefully, you get the idea. The discord
about the strudel spices up what would otherwise
be a rather monotonous scene in which Lezak gives
us the necessary background information.

79

It's actually a pretty good little script, if I do say so myself. Very Damon Runyon in its approach. Maybe somebody will film it some day and you'll be able to see for yourself.

One common mistake that writers make in delivering their exposition is to incorporate it all into one long speech, and, quite often, the character is telling this to another character who already knows that information [i.e. *"Well, Joe, you recall that...."*].

An otherwise excellent film that is guilty of this infraction is **Mr. Holland's Opus**. About twenty minutes into the picture, Richard Dreyfuss tells his wife how music became so important to him.

This is *his wife*. They've been married for awhile. Hasn't he ever told her this before?

Four points to guide you in writing good exposition.

1. Break up that exposition.
2. Give it to us in bits and pieces.
3. Deliver the speech to a character who is not already aware of its content.
4. *Delay* giving it to us as long as possible. Let us get involved in the story before you stop the forward action to explain what's happening.

Remember **North by Northwest**?
It is well into the picture. Cary Grant has

already been kidnapped and has escaped. Neither the authorities, nor his mother, believe his fantastic story. The spies are still after him, thinking he is somebody else, and, now, the police are chasing him as a suspect for a murder he did not commit.

At this point, the scene shifts to Washington D.C., where Leo G. Carroll explains to a group of government types (and us), exactly what is going on.

As I recall, it was a rather long expository speech that Mr. Carroll gave, but by that time, we were primed to know what was going on.

Sometimes, there is no valid way to avoid delivering your exposition, except in a long speech. In these cases, try to make the discourse entertaining in itself. Inject humor. Anecdotes. This helps your particular audience stay interested.

Another way to handle exposition is *via a voice over* (v.o.) narrator, a method which works well in films or stories of nostalgia or memory. Two popular movies using this technique are **Summer of '42** and **The Prince of Tides**.

Then, there is the *flashback*.

That's when you begin your story at the end...or very close to it.

Flashbacks are used effectively in such pictures as David Lean's **Doctor Zhivago**, Preston Sturges' **The Great McGinty** and John Cromwell's **Dead Reckoning**. This last example is a classic example in which an on-the-run Humphrey Bogart relates the entire plot to a priest.

In these films, except for the framing story (i.e. the opening and resolution), the entire film is presented in flashback.[2]

Another efficient way to utilize the flashback is well illustrated in movies like *Citizen Kane* and *The Killers*. Both films utilize an "Investigator."

In Orson Welles' *Citizen Kane*, the "investigator" is shadowy William Alland, a news reporter checking out the life of the late Charles Foster Kane. In **The Killers**, Edmond O'Brien is an insurance investigator seeking to solve the murder of Burt Lancaster. In both movies, the "investigator" is looking into past events, and these incidents are presented to us in fragments as he learns about them.

An offshoot of this method is the core of the great Japanese film, *Rashomon*, which has several characters relating the same past event, but from their own unique viewpoint.

One of the most brilliant uses of a flashback that I've ever seen is in the four hour version of Sergio Leone's great gangster epic, *Once Upon a Time in America*, a film of memory that jumps back and forth in time to solve a very engrossing mystery.

On the other hand, an improperly utilized flashback can spell "disaster" for a picture. The Humphrey Bogart WW2 film, *Passage to Marseilles*,

---

[2] In **Dead Reckoning**, the final confrontation also takes place after the flashback.

takes on a flashback-within-flashback structure, resulting in total confusion.

A final word of caution about this story-telling device: Be careful about adding them to the "middle" of a story, because if the flashback doesn't, in itself, advance the plot, any momentum you have working for you, is going to stop...*dead.*

Certainly the prefered way to handle exposition scenes or speeches is to avoid them altogether. Get the vital information to your reader/viewer through action or conflict.

For example, in the opening scene of **North by Northwest,** we learn all we need to know about Cary Grant via his instructions to his secretary, while they rush from his office building, grab a cab, and head to his business appointment at a nearby hotel.

Reservoir Dogs[3] begins with a bunch of guys in suits, possibly salesmen, sitting around a table in a coffee shop, chatting about porno movies, women and whether or not they should tip the waitress. In this short, seemingly ad-libbed, scene, we get a handle on each of their characters.

They leave the restaurant, walking away in a slow motion shot, while the credits roll.

Then, suddenly, there is a dramatic cut to two of the men inside of a speeding car. One of them lies in the back seat, screaming in pain. He has been shot in the gut. Blood is everywhere.

---

[3] This powerful, well written, superbly acted 1992 film contains scenes of extreme violence, as well as a considerable amount of foul language. It is not recommended for the squeamish.

As the driver of the car (Harvey Keitel) tries to calm the wounded man, we learn from their dialogue that they, and their companions, have just taken part in a robbery that has gone awry.

There's no direct exposition here. Just characterization and action. Yet, everything we initially need to know about these people and what they've done is revealed in these two scenes.

Witness does the same thing, but in a quieter, less offensive and more visual manner. The film begins with a series of shots to acquaint us with the Amish lifestyle, followed by a scene at a funeral. We meet the widowed heroine and her son; watch them depart on a train to visit her sister. Indeed, with only a few lines of dialogue, we get to know this woman and her child. More importantly, we care about what happens to them.

It's not until *after* the murder in the men's room at the Philadelphia railroad station that we learn more specific information about the characters.

◆ ◆ ◆

EXERCISE: 7 . . . .

I'm sure you can guess your assignment for this chapter. Write a scene or two of exposition, in which the information is delivered via action or character development, rather than through an expository speech.

X

OPENINGS

First impressions are vital to any good story.

That's important to know in storytelling, as well as in life.

When you're writing a novel or a screenplay, you've got to grab your reader/viewer's attention right away, or you're liable to lose him.

Aside from capturing the interest of your audience, your opening paragraph or scene has another important function.

It sets the mood or tone for your entire work.

Let's re-examine *Gone With the Wind*.

That classic film begins with a series of images, presented under the credits, of plantation life in the old South:

Slaves working in the cotton fields.

Horses grazing in the meadow.

The Mississippi.

Blossoms on a tree.

An old mill.

One of those great David O. Selznick orange sunsets.

Then, finally, the plantation house, Tara, and that memorable on-screen inscription that reads:

> *There was a land of Cavaliers and*
> *Cotton Fields called the Old South....*
>
> *Here in this patrician world the*
> *Age of Chivalry took its last bow....*
>
> *Here was the last ever to be seen*
> *of Knights and their Ladies Fair,*
> *of Master and of Slave....*
>
> *Look for it only in books, for it*
> *is no more than a dream remembered,*
> *a Civilization gone with the wind....*[1]

Even without those poetic words, the overall image on the screen is one of a peaceful, unworldly way of life; a stark contrast to the Civil War violence that will soon destroy it.

A few years back, I wrote an action/comedy screenplay that began with an amusing scene in which the hero and heroine meet.

[1] © 1939 Selznick International Pictures, Inc.; renewed 1967 Metro-Goldwyn-Mayer, Inc.

I was happy with the way that opening worked, so I continued writing the first 20-25 pages, until I realized that there was nothing in my story, thus far, to indicate that this was going to develop into a melodrama.

I'd left no clues along the way.

I went back to the beginning, but decided to leave my initial scene untouched. Instead, I added a prologue. I wrote two new scenes, played without dialogue, which showed our heroine interacting with one of the story's lead heavies, her boy friend, and a third character, whose body is dumped out of a car in the second brief scene.

That short, pre-credit sequence set the basic tone of my script. I could now move on to my comedy courtship, knowing that once we switched back to the melodramatic aspects (i.e. a second murder), the audience would not be caught off-guard.

Incidentally, as with plotting, it's not important that your audience know the significance of your opening scenes early on...just as long as they understand them by the time the final credits roll.

In **Marathon Man**, for example, we are kept totally in the dark as to the significance of the blazing, deadly automobile crash that opens the picture. The audience also has no idea why Roy Scheider is in Paris and what Laurence Olivier is doing in South America. Yet, as the film develops, the meaning of these early sequences fall neatly into place.

Less confusing, yet still a bit of an enigma at first, is the opening western sequence in **Romancing the Stone**. It takes us a few minutes to realize we've been watching a dramatization of romance novelist Kathleen Turner's latest story.

Sometimes, you can begin a story one way, then, suddenly, catch your audience by surprise and switch direction.

The perfect example of this is Alfred Hitchcock's **Psycho**. What begins as classic *film noir*, quickly changes, after the legendary shower scene, into an entirely different kind of motion picture that would later become the inspiration for many, less exemplary, slasher efforts like the **Friday the 13th** series.

I once utilized a similar switch in a story, entitled **Phantom Witness.**[2]

My "hero" is a small-time crook, who, in the opening scenes, escapes being caught in an F.B.I. "sting" operation. Racing through the streets of downtown Dallas, with an F.B.I. agent on his heels, he is struck by a car...and "dies."[3]

While "dead," he has an out-of-body experience that sends him backward in time, where he witnesses a Mafia killing. He sees the shooter, *and recognizes* him as a man who is, today, running for governor of California.

---

[2] As yet, unproduced.

[3] You will, of course, remember that we call this the "Catalyst."

Brought back to "life" by paramedics, our hero now decides to pursue this vision to see if it truly has a basis in fact, and can result in a personal profit.

Thus, what begins as essentially a cops-and-robbers piece, shifts into a psychic mystery.

The script for *Ghost,* incidentally, does essentially the same thing with its hero as I did with mine in *Phantom Witness*, except the lead character, Patrick Swayze, remains dead.

Major story switches like these are employed most effectively as either your Catalyst, or, in the case of *Psycho,* as your First Turning Point.

One popular way of beginning a story is to show your hero or heroine at a crisis point. The James Bond and Indiana Jones movies are perfect examples of this method, since they usually open with an edge-of-the-seat action sequence, signifying the conclusion of our hero's previous (unfilmed) adventure.

Star Wars is another movie that certainly begins at a crisis point: Princess Leia's space ship is about to be invaded by Darth Vader's forces.

In *Dances With Wolves*, Kevin Costner has been shot in the foot and the doctor wants to amputate. Rather than living life as a cripple, Costner decides to commit suicide by exposing himself to enemy fire.

Remember, you can always begin with a story with violent action: a robbery, a murder or a bombing that will, ultimately, involve your hero in the action and, in most cases, provide the starting point for the film's principal storyline. Orson Welles' *Touch of Evil*, *Mississippi Burning, Dirty Harry, Shoot to Kill*, and innumerable other cops and robbers movies have successfully kicked off in this fashion.

◆◆◆

EXERCISE: 8 . . . .

Your assignment: Write an opening scene that will not only set the tone for your entire work, but will also leave us wanting to read more.

XI

ENDINGS

Your final scene is approaching.

You have a decision to make.

How is your story going to end?

Actually, if you've listened to my advice and been doing your job right, you knew the answer to that long ago.

At least, in general terms.

But, then, maybe you've been winging it, or, perhaps your characters have taken on a life of their own and are attempting to write an ending other than the one you've had in mind.

Indeed, if that's the case, then go with it, because, more often than not, these fictional people that we create know more than we do.

Like a good opening, which captures your audiences' attention and sets the mood for your entire work, a good ending will tie up all loose story points and leave a final message or feeling about your material that will remain with the reader or viewing audience.

Sometimes, with pictures like *It's a Wonderful Life* or *Field of Dreams*, that message will stay with a viewer for years, and even alter his/her life.

Then, there are movies that they can't recall while munching on a hamburger thirty minutes after they've left the theater.

Since not all movies or books aspire to greatness, either one of those reactions is okay. I've been *entertained* by many films in a darkened theater that, a day or two later, I couldn't tell you what it was about.

What truly angers me though is when I see a film, good or bad, and I walk out of the theater feeling that the ending was dishonest.

What's a dishonest ending?

If your hero is surrounded by an army of bad guys ready to blow him away, and, all of a sudden, he rips open his shirt to reveal that he's wearing a Superman suit underneath, that's a dishonest ending.

On the other hand, if it's been previously established that this guy's name is Clark Kent, then it's okay.

Movie studios employ dishonest endings when their film doesn't test well at the first couple of previews.

Indeed, *Fatal Attraction*, that ground-breaking 1987 thriller with Michael Douglas and Glenn Close, had an entirely different, more downbeat, conclusion when it was first presented to audiences. The viewers didn't respond well to that ending, and a new, less intriguing ending, [one from the "slasher" school of storytelling] was written, shot and substituted.[1]

Authors employ dishonest endings after they've written themselves "into a corner," and can't figure out a way to resolve their situation.

Perhaps the classic example of this is a 1944 Fritz Lang film, *The Woman in the Window* with Edward G. Robinson and Joan Bennett. This riveting melodrama has Robinson innocently involved in a murder, and placed in the unique position where he can watch the investigation of the crime unfold. When it looks as if the police are about to arrest him, he chooses suicide over disgrace.

And, it's at this point, after Robinson has taken the deadly poison, that the writers "chicken" out. Finding no believable way to tack a happy ending onto their story, they bypass the final confrontation and have Robinson, simply, wake up. He has *dreamed* the entire movie.

Another popular picture utilizing this same dishonest device is the 1953 science-fiction cult classic, *Invaders from Mars*, which concludes with the young boy (Jimmy Hunt) waking up and realizing that his realistic[2] encounter with the evil Martians had been a nightmare.

---

[1] A home video version of **Fatal Attraction** is currently available which includes both endings.

[2] *Actually, not too realistic.* I first saw **Invaders from Mars** when I was 12, and I still recall that the frog-like Martians had zippers down their backs.

Foreshadowing:

Surprise endings in your story are okay. In fact, they're great...particularly in mysteries...just as long as you foreshadow or hint at them as your plot progresses.

Your audience or reader doesn't have to see the surprise coming, but after you've sprung it on them, they must be able to look back at what they've previously seen or read and realize that there were clues dropped along the way, and that they simply missed their significance.

When Anthony Perkins was revealed as the killer in *Psycho*, I was taken totally by surprise, yet the indications pointing to his guilt were all there. I, and most of the audience, did not pay attention to them, having bought into Hitchcock's red-herring about the mother.

Likewise, **Suspect**, the 1987 courtroom thriller starring Cher, contains a major surprise revelation as to the real killer's identity. Erroneous leads are in abundance. Yet, again, the important clues along the way are there...if slightly more elusive than in Hitchcock's film.

Endings or resolutions should be as brief, and follow as close on the heels of your final confrontation, as possible. Otherwise, your story will drift and become anti-climatic.

How many times have you seen a movie that you thought was terrific, then it went on and on, never quite knowing when to end. **China Seas**

(1935) starring Gable and Harlow, *The Mark of Zorro* (1940) with Tyrone Power[3] , Spielberg's *Hook* (1991) with Dustin Hoffman and Robin Williams and even *The Prince of Tides*[4] (1991) suffer from this kind of excess.

Also, during your story's final moments, it's not a good idea to introduce new elements into the mix. As I've said, endings are for wrapping up what has come before.

Should your ending be a "happy" or an "unhappy" one?

Certainly, "happy" is much more uplifting to an audience and a reader and, therefore, more commercial, but, in this writer's opinion, it's more important to keep an ending honest.

I recall that, as a kid, watching writer Richard Matheson's science-fiction thriller, *The Incredible Shrinking Man*, I thought all along: "If he (the hero) gets any smaller, they won't be able to inject him with an anecdote at the end of the picture and save him."

[3] In a marvelously staged sword fight, Power (Zorro) kills lead heavy Basil Rathbone 10-15 minutes before the end of the picture. That was a mistake on the part of the writers, because Rathbone was the only serious threat to Power and his followers. True, J. Edward Bromberg subsequently discovers that Power is, indeed, Zorro and throws him into prison, however the audience knows that Bromberg is a buffoon, and that his entire army is no match for our hero, who, with the help of his friends, quickly escapes and saves the day.

It would've been far more suspenseful to kill off Bromberg early, and let Rathbone stay alive until the final confrontation

[4] Others disagree with me on this film, but I've always contended that everything following Nick Nolte's dramatic revelation in Barbra Streisand's office is anti-climatic, including their subsequent affair.

Well, three cheers for Richard! He didn't chicken out. He kept the guy shrinking...to infinity. The film, as a result, has become one of the all-time classics of the genre.

Another powerful thriller that stayed honest was **Fail Safe**, Sidney Lumet's film of nuclear Armageddon that ended with the President (Henry Fonda) ordering Air Force General Dan O'Herlihy to drop two atomic bombs on New York City.

On the other hand, much has been written about how Orson Welles' masterpiece, **The Magnificent Ambersons**, was destroyed when the studio cut its original downbeat ending and substituted a more uplifting new one.

On a personal note, I recall a heated debate with the producer of **Cheyenne Warrior** (1994), my screenplay that was filmed by Concorde/New Horizons starring Kelly Preston, as a widowed pioneer woman, and Pato Hoffmann in the title role.

This story, set on the Great Plains during the American Civil War, centered upon a romance between these two diverse characters which, because of the times, could, realistically, only conclude with their parting.

The producer, however, wanted a happy ending. He wanted Kelly and Pato to stay together and marry.

Thankfully, I was able to talk him out of that idea.

Indeed, of all my scripts that have been produced, the final version of **Cheyenne Warrior** is, for me, the most satisfying.

Kelly Preston and Pato Hoffmann co-starred in **Cheyenne Warrior** (1994), a romantic western, set on the Great Plains during the Civil War.

Finally, after you've typed "The End" onto your manuscript, take another look and ask yourself our version of Ronald Reagan's favorite question: "Is my hero/heroine better or worse off than he was when the story began?"

In other words, good or bad, has their been a change in his/her status? Has he/she progressed (or regressed) from A to Z?

If the answer is in the negative, then you had better take another look at your story and its structure, because, without *some kind of change* in the central character(s), no drama has really taken place.

XII

SOME RANDOM CLOSING THOUGHTS

Many years ago, while I was still waiting to sell my first script, I asked a friend, Jack Miller, how to go about breaking into Hollywood as a writer. Jack, who is now deceased, had amassed an impressive list of movie and television credits, and was then the story editor on "Gunsmoke."

I've never forgotten his response: "Write a movie script. Make it your best work. Then, circulate it around to producers...directors... story editors...anybody in a position to help you.

"They may not buy *that* script. They may not even like the story. But, if it's well written and *they* know *their* business, they'll remember you, because good writing is good writing, and you can't hide that."

Writing is not an easy business.

Even though I had seven books published, written a monthly column for a major national magazine, and had three of my stage plays produced in the Los Angeles area, it took me ten years before I sold a screenplay, and it was another two years after that before a buyer was found for another one.

Perseverance is, indeed, the name of this game.

But, writing is an addiction. Those of us who are afflicted with the need to tell stories are without hope. We *have* to write.

Sometimes, I think it would be easier to cure oneself of a drug addiction than the need to write.

If, like me, you are cursed, make things a little easier on yourself. Give into it, and:

- Keep a notebook of your thoughts and ideas.
- Develop a visual memory of people, places, incidents and things.
- Write every day...even if you're just revising what you wrote the day before.
- Work in a way that feels comfortable to *you*.
- When you're writing your first draft, let the feelings and words flow. You can always edit later.

Finally, I'm reminded of another Jack Miller lesson. "Stick to it," he said. "Finish that book or screenplay.

"If you *don't* finish it, it will *never* sell. However, if you do complete it, there's always a chance that it might someday find a buyer."

After these words of wisdom, all I can add is:

Go out into the world, now, and WRITE!

APPENDIX 1

SELLING YOUR SCREENPLAY
One Writer's Approach[1]

So, you've finished writing your first (or, second, or third, or tenth) screenplay! Congratulations!

I'll bet you've followed all my instructions, typed it in the proper screenplay format, endowed it with about 120 pages, and it's certainly the greatest script to come down the pike since *Casablanca* and *Gone With the Wind*.[2]

Now, what are you going to do with it?

You could send it out unsolicited to Warner Brothers, Paramount or one of the other major or minor studios, but they'll just send it back...unread.

You could try to get an agent to represent you, but unless you've got major credits, he's not going to be interested either. After all, he's got plenty of well known clients for whom he can't find jobs.

1. This monograph was previously sold by the author through advertising in "Writers Digest", "Movieline" and other publications.
2. If it's not quite on a par with those classics, you'd better re-read the previous text.

True, some minor agent, or newcomer, might take you on...if he needs to enlarge his client roster. But, that's not going to do you much good. If he doesn't have prestige clients (and, if he does, he doesn't need you), then all he's going to be able to do for you is submit your screenplay to the studio story department where some reader, often a recent college graduate with pretentious ideas on what makes a good script, will write a negative coverage report, then send it back to your agent with form letter attached.

After all, that is the foremost purpose of a story department: to politely reject scripts.

A few years ago, a story editor at Columbia admitted to me that in the two years she'd been there, not one script that was first seen in the story department ever made it to the screen.

No, an agent is not going to *find* you your first deal...or even your second or third. They don't *find* deals until you get "hot."

In fact, you don't even need an agent yet. True, they can come in handy[3] , but they're not a necessity until you actually have a buyer. Once you have one of those, virtually any agent will be happy to negotiate the deal for you, in exchange for their standard 10% commission.

Fact: Just because a screenplay is good...or even great...doesn't mean that it's going to sell.

---

3. It is easier to submit through an agent, primarily because production companies will not usually require a release form if they get a script from a licensed agent. Sometimes, a smaller agent, with whom you're not officially signed, will submit a script for you after you have done the hard work and found somebody that wants to read it. Naturally, if the script sells, they get their 10%.

I wrote screenplays for ten years before I sold my first one. And, I not only had an agent, but most producers, directors, and other industry people liked my work. They praised my writing technique, my characters, my dialogue, but they just didn't want to buy my stories.

All that praise with no sales got extremely frustrating. It would've almost been better if they'd said: "You stink, kid! Go do something else."

Then, after all that time, it occurred to me what the problem was. Whether my script was good or bad wasn't the prime concern of the studios. They were more interested in "the deal."

What were the "elements" attached to the script? Who was the director? The stars?

In other words, these studio big shots were just as lazy as all the agents who don't want to find a deal. These guys (and gals) wanted me to put the elements of the picture together for them.

A perfect illustration: After I'd made a couple of sales and even had a film produced, I wrote a script that a lot of people liked and convinced my agent to send it over to the representatives of an up-and-coming, but not yet "hot" actor. Word came back that, subject to negotiating an acceptable deal, the actor, who we'll call "Joe," would like to do the role.

About the same time, I had a meeting with two independent producers located on the Columbia Pictures lot who'd read some of my work, including this particular script, and wanted to know what else I had to offer. When I asked them about the script in question, they said that whereas they'd enjoyed it, they weren't interested in producing it...until I mentioned that Joe was interested.

Immediately their attitude changed. They got on the phone that day and started pitching my project all over town. One major studio got extremely interested in the idea of doing my script with Joe. The project was approved by all of the production and creative vice presidents right up to the head man.

I'll never forget that weekend that the studio boss was going to read my script. Dreams of what color Mercedes I was going to buy continually filled my head.

Unfortunately, the big man passed. He said he'd liked the script, and the the actor; but, since he had just assumed the reins at this studio, he wanted to change the kind of films they were making. This type of movie did not fit into the new image he had in mind.

True, this story has a negative ending. But, it could just as easily turned out the other way.

The point is that, by attaching an "element," or star, to my script, it got action. Studio big shots read it, liked it and, for a short period of time, it was in the ballgame.

That's what you have to do to sell your script.

You need an element...or, better still, a "motor."

What's a motor?

A motor is a producer, director or star who likes your script so much that *they* will run with it and take it to the studio or other money people for consideration. After all, they have the clout that you don't.

That's how I sold my first script.[4]

I'd been an independent Hollywood publicist for years, and one of my clients was Abe Vigoda (**The Godfather**, TV's "Barney Miller," etc.).

I wrote a great leading role for Abe in a script called **Keaton's Cop**. He liked it so much that he arranged for me to send the screenplay to an independent producer-director that he'd recently made a film for in Texas. The guy liked it and decided that he wanted to make it. Slightly over a year later, the script went before the cameras.

Keaton's Cop starred Lee Majors, Abe Vigoda and Don Rickles, and was released by Cannon Pictures in 1990. I wasn't very happy with the final result[5], but that's another story. The important thing is that it got made and I got a "hard" film credit, which has led to other writing jobs and screenplay sales.

And, it *got* made because an actor liked a role, then used his clout to get a producer, who, in turn, became the film's "motor."

"But, wait a minute," you say. "You're already in the film industry. You already *have* Hollywood contacts. I'm just a secretary in Toledo, Ohio. What do *I* do?"

---

4. Actually, it was the 7th or 8th I'd written.
5. Neither were the critics, who uniformly blasted it. The movie had a short regional release, then went to home video and, later, played for over a year on Showtime and The Movie Channel. Indeed, I've earned more money in residuals than the film made in the theaters.

Abe Vigoda played retired mobster Louie Keaton in the action/comedy, **Keaton's Cop** (1990), which was meant to be a geriatric cop/buddy movie, in the tradition of **48 Hours**.

Believe it or not, it's not that hard to get a script to a star.

Forget about Schwarzenegger, Cruise or Costner. They're booked for the next ten years.

Think smaller. How about somebody who's the star, or second lead, on a popular television series?

Often these performers are looking to do features... either theatrical, on television or on cable. But, they never get the scripts first.

Or, maybe there's a good actor already in theatrical films, always playing the 2nd or 3rd lead, who would "kill" to star in his own picture.

Look for your "motor" in this huge pool of talent. Make a list of the actors, or, for that matter, directors, who would be right for your project, then go after *them*.

You can find out how to reach them by contacting the Screen Actors Guild or Screen Directors Guild in Los Angeles[6], and asking who is their agent. Or, perhaps your local library has a current copy of *The Players Directory*, published by the Academy of Motion Pictures Arts and Sciences. That directory, which comes out several times per year, will give you the agency information about performers.

Armed with the name of a performer or director's representative, you write to that actor or director, c/o the agency, however you mark the envelope "PERSONAL AND CONFIDENTIAL, PLEASE FORWARD." That way, you can be almost sure that the performer will get your letter, in which you will briefly describe your script, what it could do for the actor's career, and ask him to read it. Depending on how much work he has "on his plate," will determine on how likely it is that he/she will respond.

This method works. It's worked for me...more than once, and with some *very* big names.

---

6. Telephone numbers change. Get the current listings from Information. Now, of course, there is the Internet where you will find that many stars have e-mail addresses.

A few years ago, I wrote a one-man play about Orson Welles, and I felt that the perfect actor for the role was William Conrad ("Cannon"), who was then between jobs.

I called his agent and got the standard reply: "We will not submit a script to our client without a firm, play-or-pay offer."[7]

And, I knew this guy!!

So, I wrote the confidential letter to Conrad c/o the agency, and they forwarded it to him unopened. Two days later, I got a personal phone call from Conrad: "Please send me the script."

A week later, he called again. He loved the project, and I was invited over to his home where he played for me an audio recording he'd made of my play. He was brilliant in the role.

"It's a lot of work doing a one-person play," he said. "Let me think about it."

With Conrad hooked, if not reeled in, I went to a producer friend who said he could certainly get the financing for a television special, perhaps on A&E or PBS, if Conrad was aboard.

Then, unfortunately, Conrad made his deal to star in his television series, "Jake and the Fatman," and my project fell apart.

Again, the point is that I did get to the star and the deal could have just as easily gone the other way. Indeed, if Conrad had decided to do it, he could've found his own producer.

---

7. That's the Catch-22 of this business. You can't get financing for a project without a "star," but a star won't commit...or, often not even read your script, without a firm offer, which you can't give him without the financing.

That's *one* way to go about it.

Get yourself a "motor," who has industry clout, and you'll be amazed at how fast a deal can be put together.

Good Luck!

APPENDIX 2
Films to Watch

Here is a listing of most of the movies discussed in the preceding text. All are available on home video and are excellent examples of the various points discussed:

The African Queen
Alice Doesn't Live Here Anymore
Bad Day at Black Rock
Casablanca
Cheyenne Warrior*
China Seas
Citizen Kane
Dances With Wolves
Dead Reckoning
Dillinger and Capone*
Dirty Harry
Dr. Jekyll and Mr. Hyde
Doctor Zhivago
The Enemy Below
Fail Safe

Fatal Attraction
Field of Dreams
The French Connection
Ghost
The Godfather
Gone With the Wind
The Great McGinty
Guess Who's Coming to Dinner
Gunfight at the O.K. Corral
High Noon
Hook
The Incredible Shrinking Man
In the Heat of the Night
Invaders from Mars
It's a Wonderful Life
Keaton's Cop*
The Killers
Les Miserables
The Magnificent Ambersons
The Maltese Falcon
Marathon Man
The Mark of Zorro
Mississippi Burning
Moonstruck
Mr. Holland's Opus
North by Northwest
The Odd Couple
Once Upon a Time in America
One Flew Over the Cuckoo's Nest

Passage to Marseilles
The Poseidon Adventure
The Prince of Tides
Psycho
Rain Man
Rashomon
Reservoir Dogs
Rio Bravo
The Rock
Romancing the Stone
The Searchers
Shane
Shoot to Kill
Star Wars
Summer of '42
Suspect
Tootsie
Touch of Evil
The Treasure of the Sierra Madre
When Harry Met Sally....
White Heat
Witness
The Woman in the Window

*Original screenplay written by the author.

ABOUT THE AUTHOR

Michael B. Druxman is the author of (Clark) **Gable**, (Spencer) **Tracy**, (Al) **Jolson**, (Carole) **Lombard**, and **Orson Welles**, five one-person plays about show business personalities, as well as seven published books dealing with various aspects of Hollywood's past.

He wrote the original screenplay for **Keaton's Cop** starring Lee Majors, Abe Vigoda and Don Rickles, which was released to theaters in 1990 by Cannon. In addition, he penned **Cheyenne Warrior** starring Kelly Preston and Pato Hoffmann and **Dillinger and Capone** with Martin Sheen, F. Murray Abraham and Catherine Hicks, both which were produced by Roger Corman's Corcorde/New Horizons Pictures.

He also wrote episodes for **Okavango**, Gibraltar Entertainment's syndicated African adventure series starring Steve Kanaly, which airs over the Fox cable channel.

Furthermore, he has written scripts and conducted interviews for American Movie Classics; is a former monthly columnist for **Coronet Magazine**; has taught screenwriting, storytelling and creative writing at adult education universities; penned liner notes for various movies released onto laser disc; and also designed and wrote **Facts and Faces of Hollywood Greats**, a trivia game for the Macintosh.

A native of Seattle, Washington, Mr. Druxman currently resides in Calabasas, Calfornia.

Index

120

126